SHTF Prepping

Best Techniques And Strategies for Survival in Any Disaster

Jaime Baier

Table of Contents

Introduction 1

Chapter 1: Survival mindset 2

Chapter 2: Key Preparedness Principals 9

Chapter 3: Water 22

Chapter 4: Food Gathering 25

Chapter 5: Gardening 30

Chapter 6: Hunting and Fishing 39

Chapter 7: Raising Animals 43

Chapter 8: Food Preservation 46

Chapter 9: Shelter Setup 52

Chapter 10: Specific Scenarios 58

Chapter 11: Physical and Mental Ability 65

Conclusion 69

Introduction

Congratulations on downloading this book and thank you for doing so.

The following chapters will discuss preparing for survival during a disaster. Several disaster scenarios will be discussed, with detailed instructions for how to get started.

There are plenty of books on this subject on the market, thanks again for choosing this one! Every effort was made to ensure it is full of as much useful information as possible, please enjoy!

Chapter 1: Survival mindset

Some people are content living a typical life. Making sure the rent is paid, and that there is food on the table tonight is the main concern. Little thought is put into preparing for the future. Others still have a heightened awareness that should anything happen, the things they have prepared ahead of time will be crucial to their happiness, and likely, their survival.

There are lots of names for people like this, including homesteaders, preppers, and even extremists. The heavily prepared are usually thought of as a little mentally unstable, getting ready for an apocalyptic event that is unlikely to occur. If you think about it, a prepper is simply someone who realizes that our current "civilized" way of life has made most of us very complacent, content with living the way we do. Realistically, these creature comforts can be eliminated very easily, leaving the common person unable to fend for themselves, having never learned any basic survival skills.

Remember that it was only a couple centuries ago that pioneers were exploring new frontiers out west, building up pieces of formerly wild land into the civilization we see today. Heat and light came from a flame, fire wood came from tools and brute strength, and those tools came from more hard work. That's a lot of work as opposed to turning up the thermostat when it gets cold. A prepper is simply someone who realizes how lucky we have it, and figures that they should figure out what they need to do should that thermostat no longer work. They take this stance on everything: food, clean water, shelter, everything necessary for life.

The truth is, there likely will not be some earth-shattering event that changes the course of humanity in our lifetime, but it sure would be nice to know what to do if it did happen. More likely, some less-catastrophic event will happen that will rip the comfort of modern convenience away, leaving the unprepared in a bind. More and more people are beginning to realize this so prepping is a more socially acceptable, a more normal part of living.

The creed of any good prepper is to be prepared for anything and everything. This can mean dealing with a number of situations, including something so simple as losing a job. Reduced income in a household can be devastating should there be no "buffer money" or food and supplies stocked up to get the family through a hard time. This is the most common event everyone should be prepared for.

Of course, natural disasters like hurricanes, floods, wild fires and tornadoes are a step above, in some cases literally ripping the roof from over your head. Having a backup plan is absolutely essential.

Even more extreme, and much less likely, are the apocalyptic scenarios. Government collapse, nuclear war and zombie apocalypse immediately come to mind. This is the point where a lot of scoffing starts to happen, but if you plan for the worst, you will be prepared for just about anything. It is imperative for any prepper to consider all of the possible scenarios. Overlooking something can put all of their hard work in jeopardy.

The time to get ready for such an event is not when it is unfolding, but long before. Getting a plan of action in place, gathering necessary supplies for every member of your family takes time and money you may not have in times of crisis. Avoid the big questions like, "What will we eat?" and "Where do we go if…?" by doing the logistical planning ahead of time. Stress levels are high enough under these circumstances, eliminating those questions will ease your mind.

There are two types of mindsets in preppers. An every-man-for-himself attitude or a cooperative attitude. There is certainly room for being selfish in an emergency situation. Making sure you and your family have enough to eat and clean water to drink are absolutely necessary. Protecting yourself from people who want to take those things away from you is reasonable, but having a cooperative attitude will be the key to maintaining peace and building communities in the long run.

The towns and cities we have now were built on cooperation and compromise between people. Should society be degraded in a drastic way, working together will be the only way to rebuild. Ultimately, we are stronger together. We each have skills that benefit others, and sharing them makes lighter work for everybody. This is why our society works the way it does now.

Becoming fully prepared is really a commitment for the rest of your life. People dedicate days and weeks plus a great deal of money for their preparations. Admittedly, some become obsessive about it, spending their life savings and alienating themselves from family and friends to spend time on their plans. But in their minds, survival prep is the top priority.

Whether you have a few extra dollars to prep, or plan to dedicate your existence to it, there are lots of things to be done in order to be ready at a moments notice. The first step is to contemplate all of the scenarios you may find yourself in, from big to small. Simple things like stocking up on canned goods and non-perishables does a lot to prepare for just about any situation. Focus on the small things and work your way up.

Sustainable living is a huge part of prepping too. There is no way you can reasonably store enough food and water for you and your family to survive for the rest of your lives. Besides the amount of space it would take, preserved food simply does not last that long. It will be important to learn skills like hunting, fishing and growing food, so that you may sustain your life long term. Prepping is about being self-sufficient and living sustainably on the skills you have built. Make a plan to learn new skills before it is too late.

Remember, prepping is not something you do in a weekend. It is a change in your mindset that heightens sensitivity to your needs. It allows you to make small changes as you see them, gather needed supplies as they come available and make a plan of action, even if it is just a thought in your head. It is better to be prepared than to worry about your survival mid-disaster.

Chapter 2: Key Preparedness Principals

Being prepared is a multi-faceted set of skills that allows you to survive and thrive in all capacities of life. There are three main items needed for basic survival: clean drinking water, food and a shelter that provides heat. Everything else is a bonus.

Water is necessary for all life. Nothing on this planet is able to survive without it. In a temperate climate, humans can go only about three days without water. This need increases for places with low humidity or high heat, like a desert or frozen tundra. The body cannot store large amounts of water, so it must be sought out on a daily basis for survival.

Potable water, or water that is safe to drink is a strict requirement. Water could be present all around in rivers and streams, or possible all around you in a flood situation, yet it may be unsafe to drink. Just like the old saying, "water, water everywhere, but not a drop to drink", it is necessary for people to choose their water source very carefully.

Fresh water is easily contaminated by runoff coming from cities and towns. Storm drains on the street flush spilled fuel, leaking oil and other waste contaminants into the nearest running water. Water-borne bacteria call fresh water home, and they are joined by bacteria left behind in waste from animals. These contaminants are not usually seen by the naked eye, yet the consequences are steep for consuming this water.

The most common water-borne illness is dysentery. This nasty infection occurs in the intestines leading to extreme bouts of diarrhea, and in extreme cases, internal bleeding. Without proper treatment, dysentery will dehydrate you, and after too long, could actually kill you. This illness is pretty rare, except in poverty-stricken countries where clean water is unavailable.

Food is necessary to sustain the body. Without it, we would eventually die. A human can go only a few weeks without food, but is highly variable on the amount of calories needed to sustain daily activity. A person would last longer without food should they shelter in place. However, someone who is forced to move for concern over safety will last a shorter amount of time without a food supply. The effort of finding food is counterproductive in a way, because it forces the use of energy, however, it is necessary for the greater good.

As with water, a safe food supply is also needed so the body does not get infected with food borne illnesses like E. Coli or Salmonella. There are several strains of bacteria, virus and fungus that thrive in food, making it a requirement to cook most things. The longer food sits exposed to air and moderate temperatures, the faster it decomposes, and the more likely it is to contain a pathogen that will get you sick.

Methods like canning, freezing or dehydrating foods help increase the shelf life of food. Stocking up on these items and having the ability to store them is crucial to maintain a food supply. Food preservation methods will be discussed in more detail in Chapter 6.

Determining exactly how much food you will need in a survival situation is tricky, as there are several variables. Consider the following:

- How many people need to be fed?
- What are the calorie needs for each person?
- What kind of food should we be stocking up on?
- Are we sheltering in place or on the move?
- How far in the future should we plan for?

We can turn this into a pretty simple equation. Most adults can survive on less than 2,000 calories per day, especially if they are not expending a ton of energy. Assuming you stock up on canned goods, figure out how many cans of food add up to 2,000 calories, then multiply by the number of people.

How many cans needed will depend on the calorie density of the food you pick. Should you stock up on canned green beans, a low-calorie food, much more will be needed to reach the calorie goal. But if you stock up on heavy soups with proteins and fat, less will be needed to hit the calorie mark.

Storage is also something to consider. Ten cans of green beans may equal the same calories as one can of pasta and sauce, yet the pasta and sauce takes up much less space, and would be much more portable should you need to leave your home. On the other hand, a diversified food stockpile is important to make sure you are getting all of the essential nutrients you need to stay healthy.

A deficiency in any one vitamin or mineral can lead to harmful side effects. For example, having fruit on hand to maintain Vitamin C levels is needed to prevent scurvy, which causes your skin and other tissues to disintegrate and bleed. Common symptoms are bleeding gums and eye sockets. The cause of this condition was first discovered on ships bringing people to America from overseas. Passengers survived on bread and grain alone, leaving them deficient in Vitamin C. Your best bet is to include varieties of foods you eat on a regular basis so that nutrient stores can be maintained.

The big question is, "how long do we need to live like this?" Most emergency situations last only a short time, maybe two or three weeks tops. At the very least, plan to have enough to cover a small emergency, plus a few extra days as a buffer. This is a great method to use in case of a blizzard or hurricane, where you know you won't be leaving the house for at least a few days.

When starting to think ahead to more catastrophic situations, like government collapse, for example, it may be unsafe to leave your home for longer periods of time, and when you do, there may not be a stocked grocery store waiting for you. As you start to plan for the unknown, think about a number that makes you feel safe and start there. Also consider the shelf life of your stored food. Once the food is gone or expired, you will need to rely on hunting, gathering and farming for sustenance. More on that in the coming chapters.

Shelter keeps the elements out. While it is not a necessary nutrient for the body to live, shelter is required to keep body temperatures stable. While a warm bed is nice and comforting, a simple shelter that provides protection from cold, heat, wind and rain is all that is really needed.

The body must maintain a steady temperature in order to function. If exposed to extreme heat, the body temperature raises, which causes damage to vital organs. The most important organ, the brain, controls all of the other organs. When temperatures rise, cells die, causing brain damage and loss of control and function. Early signs of heat exhaustion are blurred vision and slurred speech. If temperatures increase or do not drop back to normal, more damage will occur, and could possibly lead to death.

Extreme cold has similar effects, sending the body into hypothermia. The heart slows, blood thickens and cells die from lack of oxygen. Eventually, organs shut down, leading to coma and death. Exposure to water or wind wicks away heat from the body, leading to the same result.

There are several secondary survival skills needed to maintain shelter and food and water stores. The ability to adapt to new situations and environments is crucial. Plans to stay in your current location is important, however, if moving away from where you are is needed to survive, you must plan out how you are going to do it. Consider the following:

- Where will you go?
- What can you bring with you?
- On foot or by vehicle?
- What obstacles are for seen for the journey?
- Are there different circumstances at the new location to prep for?

These questions can easily be overwhelming, especially if you begin to consider these things while an emergency is happening. Have a back up plan ready should you need to leave the house in a hurry.

Have a secondary location picked out. This can be the home of a friend or family member. Try to pick somewhere that is well out of range, so that you will not be arriving at the same disaster you just fled. The point is to escape to a safer place. For example, in a flood you would want to go somewhere where the flood waters cannot touch, a higher elevation.

If you do use a friend or family member as your backup, make sure they know you are coming. Just like an uninvited guest for dinner, they probably won't be happy to have more mouths to feed.

The journey to your alternate location could be tough, so plan for the worst. You will certainly need a vehicle for convenience. Choose something that will have enough room for everyone plus all of your gear. The vehicle should have four-wheel drive and good clearance to get over any obstacle on the road.

Make sure to have a full fuel tank and extra on board to make it where you need to go. Depending on the emergency, fueling stations will likely be destroyed or simply sold out of fuel. Make sure that the vehicle you use is in good condition. Be sure to maintain and stay on top of necessary repairs to keep rolling.

Keep a toolkit on board for repairs and tools required to move obstacles out of the road. For example, a chainsaw could be useful to clear downed trees, or a come-along pulley could help get the vehicle out should you get stuck off the road.

Act like your vehicle will be your new home. Should something happen, and your vehicle is incapacitated, it will likely be the best source of shelter. Pack blankets and bedding to maintain heat and necessary appliances to cook food. Keep a full first aid kit handy as well. Do not assume that you will make it to your desired destination, or that it will still be standing when you get there. Pack as much food and water as you can carry. Install roof racks and trunk mounts to increase storage space.

If you are lucky enough to make it to your secondary location, make sure it has the same supplies available as your primary site. Is it big enough to accommodate your entire party? Do you have a good source of food and water? The rest is secondary to basic survival.

Be ready to carry out your plan at a moment's notice. You never know when you may need to flee. Most preppers recommend having a "bug out bag" ready to go, packing crucial supplies to grab and get out. A bug out bag should include at least:

- Extra clothes
- Food
- Water
- First Aid kit and any required medications
- Radio
- Flashlight
- Map or GPS device

Also keep your car loaded with necessary supplies so little thought is needed to get going quickly. It's also nice to have it just in case the car breaks down on your way home from work.

Chapter 2 Plan of Action:

- Contemplate all possible emergency scenarios in which you need to prepare for.
- Decide how much food and water you and your family will need to survive your worst case scenario.
- Design a plan to begin gathering supplies, even if it is picking up a few extra cans at the grocery store this week. Prioritize by matter of importance to your survival.

Chapter 3: Water

Having a good source of water should be a top concern. It is easy enough to rely on city or well water on a regular basis, but that is reliant on the quality and safety of the water and having electricity to run a well pump to get it. There should always be a backup plan.

The solution for a short term emergency like a power outage is to stock up on bottled water. This is common practice for impending hurricanes or blizzards where it is likely for the power to go out. Simply but gallon jugs of water at the grocery store. Plan to have about a gallon per person, per expected day of the power outage. This water should be for drinking and brushing your teeth only.

Water will also be needed to wash dishes, clothes, and for bathing. Fill up the bathtub before an impending outage. Keep a small bucket handy to take small amounts out at a time. Do not wash dishes, clothes or yourself in the bathtub all at once, it will dirty the whole supply. Use only what you need, and use sparingly.

More long-term emergencies require more thought and planning. Bottled water does have an expiration date, usually about a year after purchase. It's likely you can get away with using bottled water exclusively for the duration of most emergencies, but having enough storage space to store enough water for the whole year is a big challenge.

A secondary source of water should be available. A local river or stream could be used, depending on possible contaminants inhabiting the water. If the only likely contaminants are bacterial or viral, boiling the water before drinking is an easy way to get fresh water. Unless electricity is available to use the stove, an alternative heat source, like a fireplace or outdoor fire pit will be needed to make this work.

Portable water filters commonly used for camping are a great tool as well.

Chapter 3 Plan of Action

- Determine how much water will be needed to sustain the entire family.
- Determine out how much can be reasonably stored.
- Find a secondary water source like a river or stream.
- Determine how to sanitize the water before drinking.

Chapter 4: Food Gathering

Once the canned goods are gone, what do you do? Unless your game plan included withering away to nothing, you will need to find food on your own. The choice to go out to find food is a tricky one, depending on your surrounding environment.

Should you be in the city, or a well-populated area, it may be easy go find more canned goods. Looking in abandoned houses or stores seems like a no brainer. However, if you have ever seen any post-apocalyptic movie, you know that the so-called 'abandoned' buildings usually aren't uninhabited. It may be unsafe to enter a place where others are hiding out, as they may feel threatened by you.

There is also a good chance that the likely food stores have already been cleaned out, leaving you empty handed, having wasted more energy trying to find food. In this scenario, it will be necessary to resort to the givings of the environment. In a city location, there may not be wild plants to feed off of, but more rural areas will provide more. Be sure to consider this when deciding to stay put or move to your secondary location during an emergency. Choosing to live in a naturally abundant place is your best bet. Avoid staying in environments with little natural vegetation, like a desert. Naturally luscious areas that experience rough winters can also become food deserts as temperatures drop below freezing.

Deciding to eat plants in the wilderness can be dangerous. You can't simply walk out into the woods and eat anything that looks tasty. That delectable wild leaf you chose could cause sickness or even death. Do your due diligence to learn to identify local plants and be able to tell them apart. Find a book that identifies edible plants to keep in your possession. Remember you likely will not be able to look things up on your cell phone during an emergency.

Be cautious of eating all parts of an edible plant. There are several species that are safe to eat only when cooked, and specific parts of the plant can be poisonous. For example, rhubarb is a crop that is grown and used all the time for strawberry rhubarb pie. The stalks are edible, but the leaves are poisonous.

Research wild edibles in your area long before any emergency situation occurs. Explore the local area for patches of safe edible plants to eat ahead of time to save time and unnecessary energy expenditure. Remember to do some reconnisiance at different times of the year, as plants bloom and wither on different schedules.

In your research, be sure to find out what times of year certain plants can be harvested. For example, in an environment where wild berries grow, the picking season can run through late summer, but a wild strawberry patch specifically produces fruit only in early July. Once the fruit has gone by, this becomes an unusable source.

The best time to begin foraging for food is now. Learning how to find and prepare safe edibles is a crucial skill to build over time. While in an emergency situation, don't wait until your food supply is gone to begin your search. It's a good idea to find what you can and use it to supplement your stored foods as things become available. As foraged supplies dwindle, go back to canned goods as a backup.

Chapter 4 Plan of Action

- Find a book containing identification and preparation information on natural edibles specific to your location. Must be tangible paper copy!
- Make a list of possible plants to look for, noting what times of year they grow or produce fruit. Ideally, have an option for all times of the year.

- Explore the local area to find places where edible plants grow.

Chapter 5: Gardening

One step above foraging for food is growing it yourself. Having an abundance of food readily available on your property is good for a number of reasons. You will likely be able to grow more food than you can find, and it will not take as much energy to find it on a daily basis. Yes, a good amount of time and energy will be needed to get a garden going, but as the season continues, less is needed to maintain it.

Just like foraging for food, planning a garden will require some prep work as well. Most people are not born with a green thumb, growing is a skill that develops over time. Start to increase your skills now to avoid making crucial mistakes when your life could be on the line.

Research plant species and varieties that grow well in your environment. Most landscapes have a growing season for at least a few months of the year. Common high-producing crops like summer and winter squash, tomatoes, and leafy greens grow easily in most climates and provide lots of nourishment with little effort. Don't put all of your eggs in one basket. It is common for one type of plant, for example, tomatoes, to do very well one year, then produce nearly nothing the next.

The amount of crop produced is highly variable, and depends on temperature, rainfall, and pest infestation. Plants can be quickly overtaken by insects, or eaten whole by woodchucks or deer in one day. Mold can take over rain is a large part of the forecast. Have a diversified variety of plants increases your chances of having some success, even if not all of the plants thrive.

Do your best to prevent any of these variables from taking over your garden. Fencing can be put up to keep large critters like deer and raccoons out. Be sure the fence is tall enough for large enough, and is set into the ground to prevent animals that dig from getting under.

Products like pesticides can be used in case of bug infestation. Natural options like diatomaceous earth is also available as an organic method. Be sure to monitor your plants, remembering to turn leaves over to check for bugs. Treat your plants as needed. Certain aromatic plants like mint, oregano and marigolds can be planted around crops to naturally repel bugs.

Unfortunately, you can't predict or prevent excess rainfall, but you can make sure your garden is in a place that does not gather water. The ideal location for planting is on a slight slope near the top of a hill, so that water runs off preventing pooling. The garden should get sunlight for a good part of the day, both for plant growth, and to make sure excess water can evaporate before mold can grow.

As discussed with canned food, having a variety of vegetables and fruit will prevent nutrient deficiency. Grow a variety of starchy and non-starchy vegetables to act as both a vegetable and a source of carbohydrates. Winter squashes like butternut, pumpkin and spaghetti are very starchy and filling. They also have tough skins that preserve the inside of the vegetable for long periods of time, often lasting in storage through late fall.

Fruit should also be considered as a crop, yet is usually tougher to grow. Ground-dwelling varieties like strawberries quickly multiply, however, it takes a few seasons to develop a large patch, and the yield becomes high. Varieties like blueberries and apples, that grow as bushes and trees take much longer to establish and produce fruit. Should you want to rely on these fruits to survive, now is the time to begin planting them, since they will not produce much for a few years.

A garden cannot grow without seeds. It is simple enough to run down to the garden center to pick up seed packets, or even seedlings started in the greenhouse. It does take some skill to grow plants from seed, so make sure to try it, as you may not be able to rely on that garden center should you be living under different circumstances.

Every plant will produce a seed, whether it be a part of its fruit, like in cucumbers or zucchini, or as part of the flower, like in leafy greens. In your research, learn to identify seeds, and for how long the plant needs to live to form them. Start collecting seeds as you go through the growing season to start new plants and to save for next season. Seeds can be easily dried in the sun, then stored in a cool, dry place until they are needed. You can also simply buy extra seed packets at the store, however, if they are stored too long, they may not produce. It is better to collect fresh seeds on a yearly basis so your stores stay fresh.

Many people use their well water and a garden hose to keep plants watered, but you must consider that you may not have this as an option. Just like with drinking water, try to find a secondary source to use for garden watering. It could be as simple, yet as inconvenient as using buckets to collect water from the stream out back. This method could get tiring, and cause of excess energy expenditure. Consider building a hosing system with pumps run on solar or water power to transport water across the terrain to the garden.

The growing season can be extended by several weeks, increasing your yield. First, start seeds inside well before the season begins. Use seed kits and potting soil to get seeds going. Stagger planting your seeds to prevent all of the plants from producing at once. This gives you more time to eat the fresh produce or decide to preserve it. Wait about two weeks between plantings to start new seeds. By the time the first crop peters out, the second should be ready to go.

Make sure to leave extra space to plant new seeds throughout the season. There are many techniques for planning and designing your garden. Do some research to make sure you do not overcrowd your plants, and give them the best growing environment as possible. Your dedication to this step will be rewarded later in the season.

Specific directions are on the back of your seed packets. Plants should be well established and ready to be planted at the time of last frost. Planting too early subjects the gentle seedlings to freezing, which they likely won't make it through. This date depends highly on location. Check a farmers almanac to determine your zone and normal growing season. A few plants, like snow peas and kale can be planted outside early, as they are more hearty in frost.

The growing season can be extended past frost by planting heartier plants like lettuce, broccoli and kale later in the season. Plants can also be covered with plastic or cloth on nights where frost is imminent to keep them warm. Also insulate them with grass clippings or hay around the base to keep the warmth in the soil.

The prospect of gardening as a source of food can be an overwhelming task, so it is better to build up some basic skills now to be prepared when it is a necessity to live. Having practice over several seasons can help you determine how much yield is average out of each plant, and you will be able to gauge how many plants to sow in order to get specific yields. The goal should be to have enough fruits and vegetables to eat year round. More on storage of the fruits of your labor in Chapter 8.

Chapter 5 Plan of Action
- Start refining gardening skills
- Test grow fairly hearty plants like zucchini or lettuce to learn watering, fertilizing and pest prevention skills.
- Build on skills in the future by trying new varieties and more difficult plants.

- Figure out how many plants will be needed to provide a good yield that will last all year round.

- Remember to save seeds!

Chapter 6: Hunting and Fishing

The majority of people eat meat, and rely on store-bought cuts of meat. Just like canned fruits and vegetables, canned meats like tuna fish, chicken or beef has an expiration. Besides, it's certainly not the tastiest way to eat meat. Canned goods will serve their purpose in a survival situation, but eventually, it will run out.

Hunting and fishing will be necessary to maintain protein in the diet. It is a great source of energy, and is essential to maintain muscle stores in the body. It is also a great source of iron and B vitamins, which are needed for energy production and nerve function. It packs more calories per ounce than any vegetable ever could, so it is ideal to keep as a survivalist food.

Like gardening, hunting is an acquired skill, something to develop over time. Many people choose not to hunt because of ethical reasons, but others prefer to get their own meat, so they know where it comes from.

If you are new to hunting, start small. Fishing is probably the easiest start. It requires only a fishing pole and bait. Unlike hunting big game like deer, it requires little practice, it is more a waiting game. The downfall to fishing is that the quality and safety of the fish depends on the water it lives in. Should the water be contaminated with heavy metals or pollution, the fish will be as well.

Hunting small mammals like squirrels, birds or rabbits can be done using traps or a small caliber gun that requires little skill to use. If you are not used to operating a gun, a 17 or 22-caliber would be a good start. Another option would be a pellet gun, which can be used for hunting small animals, yet is easier to get used to than a gun.

Do target practice and get used to your weapon until you feel comfortable. Practice from different angles and distances to mimic any scenario. Also practice shooting quickly and accurately. Your gun can double as a source of protection, and if under duress, you will need to be able to shoot as effectively as possible to protect yourself.

Remember that killing an animal is not the end of the story. Do your research and learn how to properly clean and skin the meat before you even shoot. Find out how to use every piece of the animal so nothing goes to waste. Most meat needs time to rest and set before it can be cut. The muscle fibers need to relax and the blood needs to set. The time this takes to happen depends on the size of the animal. Invest in a book explaining rest times as well as cleaning tips to use as a reference.

Make sure to treat your gun like the tool it is. Keep it clean and oiled. Keep as much ammunition as possible, but watch posted expiration dates. It is possible to reload rounds yourself. You will need shell casings, powder and a press to do it at home.

Each round style is different, so make sure to research the proper powder amounts for each size for your safety. Extra rounds should be stored in a cool dry place.

Chapter 6 Plan of Action

- Invest in equipment for fishing and hunting
- Do required target practice to learn to use a gun
- Research how to clean and prepare your meat
- Make sure to use every bit of the animal as possible. Nothing goes to waste!

Chapter 7: Raising Animals

The unfortunate thing about hunting, just like foraging for wild edibles, is the unpredictability of supply. It is possible to walk around the woods expending energy for the entire day and not find anything. Raising animals specifically for meat can solve this problem.

It is suggested to start with raising chickens or ducks. These animals produce eggs which can be consumed immediately and regularly. Eggs provide a steady source of protein year round. As the chickens age, they can be harvested for meat as well. Having one rooster plus several hens allows them to procreate, keeping a steady roost of chickens for years on end.

The birds can be kept in a fenced in area, or can run free range. However, they are not high on the food chain and can easily attract large predators like fox, coyote or fisher cats. They should be caged in at night to protect them.

They can be fed with garden scraps like wilted lettuce and corn meal during the growing season. It is possible to dry corn to feed them through the winter months as well.

Larger animals like goats and cows provide meat, but also milk that can be made into cheese or butter as they grow. Larger animals require much more care, and certainly eat a lot more. The downfall to raising any animal is that they end up being more mouths to feed. They can graze on grass and other plants through the growing season, but will require large amounts of hay in the winter months. Just make sure to keep them out of your garden.

Be sure you are able to support the animals you decide to raise before getting them. The way you look at your animals is important as well. Remember that they are meant to be a food source, not a pet. You must be able to harvest your animal when the time comes. Give it a good life while you watch it mature, but do what needs to be done when the time comes. Learn techniques for slaughter that is the most humane, and get it done without causing unnecessary suffering in the animal. Not only is a prolonged death inhumane, excess stress hormones like adrenaline and cortisol are raised, decreasing the quality of the meat.

Chapter 7 Plan of Action

- Research the ins and outs of owning a farm animal including what they eat, living requirements and health concerns. Homesteading resources and forums are a great place to start.
- Consider visiting/working at a farm to get a handle on animal care.
- Build a chicken coop or fenced in area for desired animals.

Chapter 8: Food Preservation

You have foraged, harvested and hunted. What do you do with the fruits of your labor? Unless you preserve the food you worked hard to get, it will all go to waste. There are several methods for preservation, some of which are not appropriate for survival situations.

Food safety should be the number one priority in preservation. Exposure to bacterial or viral toxins on food can will make you very ill, and without treatment, could cause death. Take good care to make sure the food you painstakingly gathered is not the thing that kills you in a survival situation.

Refrigeration and Freezing: This is really the easiest way to store vegetables or meat. Most modern homes have a refrigerator and freezer. Meat can be portioned and stored with ease. Vegetables can be flash-steamed, packed and stored for immediate storage. Meat and vegetables stay fresh for a few days to a week in the refrigerator, but for indefinite amounts of time in the freezer. If stored frozen for more than a few months, food can get freezer burnt, giving it an off flavor, but is still safe to eat when cooked.

Unfortunately for refrigeration and freezing, they require electricity, and lots of it to run. You can assume that in an emergency, the power will be lost first, leaving your frozen foods vulnerable to spoiling. This is certainly not the best method for long-term storage.

Canning-Food sealed in jars makes them shelf stable without the need for refrigeration. The point is to eliminate all bacteria and air from the food so it will last much longer. It is the ideal storage method for long-term power outages that are likely to occur. Any food can be canned, but there are different methods to use depending on the acid content of the food. Home canned foods should be used within one year of packaging, and should be thrown out should the seal not hold.

Invest in a guide showing the proper way to can food and the proper times, temperatures and pressures for safe storage.

- **Boil only**-foods that are high acid like diced tomatoes, tomato sauce or vegetables that are pickled in vinegar are safe to boil only. Jars simply need to be sealed, and boiled under water until the jar seals. The type of food and size of the jar will dictate how long they need to boil.

- **Pressure canning**-low acid foods, like alkaline vegetables, dairy products and meat should be pressurized to kill stubborn bacteria. Jars are sealed, then placed in a pressure cooker. The cooker be brought up the proper pressure, then cook for a specified amount of time to ensure food safety. If this is not done correctly, botulism, a potentially deadly toxin, will be allowed to grow in the food.

The only downfall to canning is the need for lots of water and a heat source, likely fire, that can boil water. Pressure canning is even more difficult because the pressure in the cooker must remain constant, a task that may be difficult using an unpredictable flame. Electric pressure canners are available the regulate temperature and pressure on their own. This may be a good appliance you use your generator for.

Dehydrating and smoking- taking the moisture out of food helps prevent bacterial growth. Many commercial dehydrators are available, but require electricity to work. Meat or fruit are good candidates for dehydration. The produce can be sealed in plastic bags and stored at room temperature. Outdoor smokers could also be built to smoke fish and meat without the need for electricity. Using specific types of wood like hickory gives different flavors, however, any wood smoke will do in a pinch.

Cold Cellar- The earth beneath our feet helps provide a cold space to store vegetables. Creating a room underground will provide an environment that naturally stays cool without the need for refrigeration. All vegetables and fruits can be stored on dry grass or hay to wick moisture away. They should be rotated regularly to avoid rotten spots. Spoiling pieces should be removed regularly to avoid mold growth.

Having a variety of food storage options assures that your stores remain fresh and safe to eat. Think about having items stored outside of your main living area. Should anything happen to your home, a secondary food store will be available. Use an outdoor shed or cold cellar well away from the main living area.

Chapter 8 Plan of Action

- Pick at least two preservation methods for storing food, at least one should keep food at room temperature.
- Research, gather supplies and practice skills for food preservation
- Figure out where to keep excess food.

Chapter 9: Shelter Setup

The best case scenario in any emergency situation would be the ability to shelter in place. It is easier to plan and gather resources to keep in a place where you are already living. While ideal, preparations still need to be made to protect your home, your supplies and your family. This applies to dangers from natural elements like wind and rain, but also from people who may be out to steal things from you.

Windows and doors must be able to lock. Have supplies on hand to barricade both from the inside and outside. Plywood and screws work well in situations like a hurricane where the main need is to protect glass from breaking. If it is people you worry about, barricading from the inside will keep someone from unscrewing the plywood. Long term shelter in place will likely require more than plywood. Think about metal bars or sliding metal plates for added protection. The only downfall for this plan is these would likely need to be installed now, giving a prison-like look to your home. If you don't mind that, feel free to do it now.

Your home should be set up to work without electricity. Have a working fireplace inside and outside to use for cooking and sanitizing water. Make sure there is plenty of wood cut and ready to use. Have flashlights and candles at arms reach in every room. In certain situations, you will also want some sort of weapon for protection in reach as well. If children are in the house, make sure to secure them out of reach.

Generators come in handy to supplement electricity, but they are only good as long as there is fuel to run them. Portable gas generators are easiest to store, but a stationery propane version runs more efficiently. Propane can be stored for longer periods of time than gas. Gas, especially if sitting in the generator can expire and gunk up the system. Keep your generator in top shape by running it at least once a month to make sure it is ready to use. Fuel stabilizer can be used to increase the shelf life of your fuel, but regularly use your stocked fuel for routine things like the lawn mower to keep it from getting too old.

Whichever fuel source you decide to use, treat the generator like a luxury, because it is. Eventually, you will run out of fuel, so only turn it on when you need it run necessary equipment. Most people can survive without electric lights and television, but not medical equipment like oxygen machines. Use your resources sparingly.

There are many situations, including flood, civil unrest or war that will make it necessary to leave your home in search of a safer location. Part of your plan should be having a second location in which you can shelter in place. The problem with having another place to go so far away from the first is the distance in between.

A lot can happen while traveling. During an emergency, many more obstacles will present themselves. You need to be prepared for any scenario. Aside from natural obstacles like downed trees or treacherous roads, you must also be ready to defend yourself and be ready to abandon your vehicle and survive in the environment around you.

Be sure to pack lightweight camping gear that you can carry on your back. Have a supply of food, like jerky, that is lightweight and doesn't take up too much space. Have supplies for hunting, like a gun, and knives for cleaning meat. Bring a hatchet to cut wood and build a makeshift shelter should you need to. Most importantly, have several fire starter sources, like lighters, matches and flint. Don't forget to bring a first aid kit with you to deal with minor injuries.

Go camping often in preparation for living in the wilderness. Become confident with starting a fire, learn how to make a natural shelter, should you not have a tent. Be able to cook over a fire, and when you feel comfortable, hunting for food. As you become more comfortable, eliminate modern conveniences, like pots and pans for cooking, and learn to cook without them. Learn to work with less to decrease the amount of supplies you need to carry with you.

When traveling, wear clothes that you could survive in should you need to quickly flee your vehicle and supplies. Do not underestimate your climate. Sunny, warm days quickly turn to cold rainy nights, and, should the season change while you travel, you will not survive in light summer clothing. Avoid bright colored clothing to camouflage yourself from animals you are hunting, and keeps you safe should you need to hide yourself.

Have a GPS device or maps handy to help you get where you need to go. Map out an alternative route to your secondary location. If it is not safe to travel along a road, make sure your alternative route includes shortcuts through wooded areas that others are less likely to use. Plan this ahead of time and test it out. If this journey is predicted to take several weeks, consider having an alternative vehicle, like another truck or off road vehicle stored somewhere along the way.

If the route does not cut through your own property, you run the risk of having a secondary vehicle stolen or damaged if hidden on someone else's property. Your primary vehicle should have enough supplies to last the entire journey on foot should your secondary plan fall through.

Chapter 9 Plan of Action
- Pack your bug out bag.
- Map out the distance between your primary and secondary locations noting any obstacles.
- Consider scenarios where your vehicle is incapacitated, and you must travel on foot.
- Brush up on basic camping skill, building shelter.

Chapter 10: Specific scenarios

Hurricane or flood: Evacuate out of flood or hurricane warning zones should there be advanced warning. Take anything you can and do your best to prepare your home for the damage. Use sandbags to create a barrier for water. Move supplies and furniture to the highest level of the home to avoid water damage. Board up windows and doors to prevent high winds or water from breaking glass. Turn off gas sources before leaving. If you have animals on your property, take them with you if you can. If you cannot take large animals like horses or cows, release them so they have a chance to leave the area. Leaving them penned up almost guarantees they will not survive.

Should you decide to shelter in place, set up sandbags and board up windows as if you were leaving, but also make sure your supply of food and water is ready and out of possible flood zones. It is not a bad idea to have a small boat, life jackets or other floatation devices on hand should a flood over take you, or you need to cross water to get out. Remember that sheltering in place is your choice, and should a situation become critical, you are on your own. It would not be fair to put someone else's life in danger to save you, especially if you had the opportunity to leave.

Civil Unrest: A scenario like this can vary greatly, depending on the people around you. In recent years, groups of people have reacted to social injustices in violent ways, directly affecting the communities in which they occurred. Property destruction, damage and violence against police and other civilians destroyed entire neighborhoods. Should you be unlucky enough to live in an area where this is happening, you may be in a position where you need to defend yourself, your family and your property. Prepare to shelter in place, boarding up all possible entrances for safety. Create a look out spot in the top level, or on the roof of your home to watch for impending violence.

Should civil unrest be more widespread, say, with the collapse of a government or in a war torn area, violence and danger may not be immediately visible, but your guard should be up. As civilization declines, the likelihood of being the victim of a crime increases. People are willing to kill over food and supplies. Over prepare yourself by monitoring all windows and doors, barricade them if you feel threatened. Keep a lookout for people in your neighborhood you have never seen, and ban together with neighbors to create a better sense of security.

Nuclear or chemical warfare: This is a less likely scenario, but an extremely dangerous one. Unfortunately, if you are in the direct strike zone of a nuclear bomb, it will be unlikely you will have enough warning to get to a bomb shelter, that is, if you even have one. Should you survive the blast in an underground shelter, a nuclear winter of at least two years will coat the surface of the environment with radioactive chemicals. Exposure will likely lead to death. In this scenario, you will need to have stored enough food and water to last at least two years in an underground room. That room must have been set up with all necessary supplies like cooking supplies, generator and first aid kits.

When it is safe to leave your shelter, gas masks and protective suits should be worn to decrease radioactive exposure. Potassium iodide supplements help reduce the effects of radiation on the body. Research appropriate doses for everyone in the family, and buy accordingly. Find outerwear that is suitable for radiation, gas and biological agents to cover all of your bases.

Extreme heat: Wildfires or drought create hell-like landscapes that are difficult to survive in. Fire creates smoke, so have gas masks available. Ordinarily, humans deal with heat by wearing light colored clothing, leaving most skin exposed. In extreme heat where burn from a flame or the sun is possible, skin should not be exposed. Take a lesson from people in middle-eastern countries that wear lightweight, breathable clothing that protects the skin. In case of wildfire, if you are close enough to get burned, you will likely be in a world of trouble any way. Like hurricane or flood, you will likely have notice to leave ahead of time, which you should.

In case of wildfire, preparations can be done around the house to minimize damage. The fire runs on fuel from dry brush, trees and bushes. Keep a 50-100 foot perimeter around your home vegetation free. Create fire breaks to prevent the fire from spreading. This should all be done ahead of time, as you likely won't have time when staring a fire in the face. If there is time, grab the garden hose and douse any surface you can with water. Wet wood takes longer to burn, and if you are lucky, the fire may move on or extinguish before the water evaporates and the wood starts burning. It is not a guaranteed method, but it can't hurt, as long as you don't stay behind to do so.

Extreme cold: Have as many alternative heat sources as possible. Should you be stuck in sub-zero temperatures, you cannot rely on traditional heat sources like oil or propane which require electricity to distribute. Having a fireplace in your home is an easy alternative. Have large amounts of wood and kindling available for long periods of time. Concerns of carbon monoxide poisoning increase using wood heat as a source. Have carbon monoxide detectors set up to make sure excess carbon monoxide from smoke isn't building up in your living space.

Secondary to heat, have appropriate clothing like boots meant for temperatures below zero, wool socks, thermal pants and shirts, heavy coats, hats that cover the ears, face masks and gloves. They should be top quality since you may need to rely on them for long periods outside should you need to leave your home. If outside, have tents or sleeping bags rated for cold climates to protect yourself outdoors.

aid, things needed for specific situations, list and explain needs specific scenarios.

Any and all situations: Cash is king in emergency situations. Don't think for a second that swiping the credit card is an option during emergencies. Card machines do not work without electricity, usually the first casualty in emergency situations. Have cash on hand to buy fuel, food or other supplies. Should society completely fall apart, money will be no good, and we go back to bartering goods and services for supplies. Have popular items like food and tools on hand to barter with. Remember that skills like hunting and gardening are skills that others may not have, and could be used as a bargaining tool.

Chapter 10 Plan of Action

- Have gas masks available for all members of the family.
- Be vigilant of escalating situations, reacting quickly and efficiently with your plans.
- Keep cash on hand to buy supplies.

Chapter 11: Physical and Mental Ability

We have discussed most aspects of basic survival and homesteading, but have missed one crucial factor. You may have noticed that preparations involve learning new skills, and also require a lot of work, both physical and mental. Honestly, you will not do well if you are out of shape.

Consider how much walking, running, and lifting you will be doing as you hunt, garden and prepare wood for fires. That alone is enough to wear out a well-exercised person, let alone someone who has a desk job five days a week. It must be a priority to make physical fitness a part of your prepper routine. You are preparing for your survival. The body has natural "fight or flight" responses that create adrenaline for combat or getting out of a bad situation. You will likely lose in either situation if your body is not up for the task.

Think about how you might get away from someone who wants to harm you. Do you think you could outrun someone long distance? If your answer is no, work on it, just like you would improve on other prepper skills. Add small amounts of cardio and weightlifting to your routine, increasing the amounts as you become comfortable. The healthier you are, the more likely you will be able to survive.

Start here:

- Add 15 minutes of cardio to your daily routine. If already doing cardio on a daily basis, add more or increase bouts intensity.
- Add 15 minutes of weight training to your daily routine. This could include a combination of body weight exercises like sit ups, pushups and pull ups. Don't count daily tasks you already do. The point is to improve, not stay the same.

Mental disposition during an emergency is just as important as physical ability. How clearly you are able to think will dictate the success or failure of your plans. All of the preparations could be done, but if your mind cannot handle the stress of a survival situation, you will not make it. Practice mental toughness now. The first step is to master your survival skills to the best of your ability. Knowing exactly how you will carry on during an emergency takes an enormous stress off the brain.

Being confident that you can defend yourself, hunt for food, start a fire goes a long way. Just like knowing how to cook or pay your bills now is part of your regular life, they were once things that had to be learned. You need to normalize your new skills, so they are just a part of daily life. Now that you have mastered them, they are just another skill you have, and it doesn't take much energy for your brain to deal with these problems.

Second, practicing techniques like meditation and yoga or Tai Chi for exercise can help maintain calm and mental focus. Learn ways to deal with stress in a healthy way, using deep breathing or exercising. These techniques will help you remain calm during stressful situations. In your preparations, pack things that are soothing and entertaining. Things like books, puzzles and toys for kids can help preoccupy the mind, even if only a temporary escape from the situation. It may be just enough to make it through.

Conclusion

Thank for making it through to the end of this book, let's hope it was informative and able to provide you with all of the tools you need to achieve your goals whatever they may be.

The next step is to put your plans into action. There was a lot of information proposed here, so start small. Pick a few things to work on and master some new skills.

Finally, if you found this book useful in anyway, a review on Amazon is always appreciated!

www.ingramcontent.com/pod-product-compliance
Lightning Source LLC
Chambersburg PA
CBHW060213290526
45789CB00003B/1250